Let's Get Talking
A Speech-Language Therapy Companion for a Child's First Functional Words

Mehreen Kakwan LLC
Ann Arbor, MI

Dedicated to my brother Mo and his Tomorrowland

ISBN: 9781090350527

Introduction

The creation of this book was inspired by the experiences I had with parents and caregivers who wanted to apply a consistent home program from their child's first day of speech-language therapy. Observing your speech-language pathologist (SLP) prompt productions in therapy can be helpful, but to fresh eyes, it's difficult to imitate the cues and outcomes in an effective way. The intention is to empower parents with insight to how your SLP makes sure the next achievable step is not too easy or too difficult. We want to ensure your child is challenged, but not frustrated. The guidance can help your child produce their first functional words and enable them to get their wants and needs met via language rather than gestures (e.g. pointing), vocalizations (e.g., crying out) and/or behaviors (e.g., tantrums due to communicative frustration).

Children who are producing fewer words than expected for their age may have either an expressive language delay or a combination of an expressive and receptive language delay. If a child also has a receptive language delay, following the directions to effectively imitate and produce sounds independently can be more challenging. An SLP can assess your child's communicative strengths and weaknesses and create the most effective treatment plan for improvement. A speech-language diagnosis may be linked to a medical condition or, for example, a motor-speech disorder like Childhood Apraxia of Speech (CAS), or a developmental disorder like Autism Spectrum Disorder (ASD). (An SLP is qualified to diagnose CAS and can offer a referral for an ASD evaluation.) Treatment plans are adjusted to meet each unique case.

The guidance outlined in this book is loosely based on the DTTC (Dynamic Temporal and Tactile Cueing) Method, an evidence-based practice for the treatment of Childhood Apraxia of Speech that focuses on imitation, as well as tactile, and auditory models. A child demonstrating an expressive language delay can also benefit from this technique, however the child will likely progress to accurate imitations more swiftly if they do not have difficulty with motor-planning, as children with CAS do. Not all children with an expressive language delay or disorder have CAS. CAS is a type of speech sound disorder characterized by specific difficulty programming the correct oral motor movements for the production of speech.

Use this guide as a complement to your SLP's home program. I encourage you to share the book with your SLP so she/he can offer customized guidance in light of your child's strengths and areas of weakness.

I wish your child a clear and successful journey to their first functional words. Write to me and share your experiences, I'm happy to hear from you!

Mehreen Kakwan, M.A. CCC-SLP
Speech-Language Pathologist
mk@mehreenkakwan.com

A Brief Introduction to Preverbal Developmental Skills
Normally developing children demonstrate these skills in their first 12-15 months

Several developmental skills create the foundation for communicative speech, before a child produces their first word. Working with language delayed children to develop these preverbal skills is an expansive area of expertise practiced by Speech-Language Pathologists (SLPs). The following list of preverbal skills is not comprehensive, rather it highlights dominant skills that must be demonstrated before a normally developing child will start producing words.[1]

Pre-verbal Skill	Description
Eye contact when establishing joint attention or when child is requesting	Child establishes attention to a speaker by making eye contact, then indicating a interest or desire by shifting gaze to the shared activity or desired object, then reestablishes the caregiver's eye contact. This behavior can communicate a shared emotion (e.g., laughing at a toy) or a desire (e.g., milk bottle that's out of reach).
Responding to sounds, when others call her by name or talk to her/him	Child demonstrates ability to respond to hearing their name, to recognize emotions in voices, and reacts appropriately (e.g., startles by loud noises, mirrors a smile and happy voice, turns gaze towards music and sounds).

[1] Laura Mize, M.A. CCC-SLP offers extensive resources regarding the development of preverbal skills. An absence of nonverbal interaction skills can indicate greater issues than late talking. See endnotes.

Pre-verbal Skill	Description
Babbling and vocalizing for attention	Child coos and babbles repetitive sounds playfully (e.g., mimi, pup, bababa) before he/she produces intentional vocalizations in order to establish attention.
Anticipation of simple cause and effect	Child anticipates simple patterns in actions, as well as understands cause and effect even when an object falls out of sight. (e.g.,When a train enters on one side of a tunnel, child looks at the other end expecting the train to reappear; child holds your gaze as you hold the bubble wand, waiting for you to blow bubbles.)
Understanding and imitating gestures	Child looks in the direction in which you point. Child imitates gestures and independently gestures as well.(e.g., points, waves hi/bye, clapping, high fives, shakes head "no," and responds to gestures in back-and-forth games.)
Following simple directions with and without gestures	Child demonstrates understanding of language by following 1-2 step simple directions, with and without gestures. (e.g., "Come here," "Throw the ball to me," "Bring me your shoes and your coat," "Want more?")

Steps in Neurotypical Speech Development

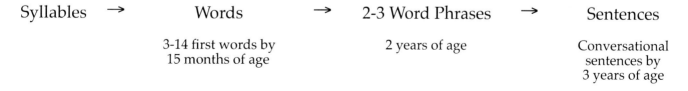

Syllables → Words → 2-3 Word Phrases → Sentences

3-14 first words by 15 months of age

2 years of age

Conversational sentences by 3 years of age

Vowel Sounds

Although the English language identifies only 5 letters as vowels (a, e, i, o, u, and sometimes y), we phonetically produce 20 different vowel sounds. Children with Childhood Apraxia of Speech (CAS) often produce distorted vowel sounds and may find more neutral vowel sounds, like "ah" or "eh," easier than "oh" or long "ee," which require more precise articulatory movements. We focus on improving the movements of the *articulators (jaw, lips, and tongue)* for syllable production and word approximations. We build towards mastery over time.

Good ways to practice imitation skills and the articulatory movements for vowels is with environmental and exclamatory sounds throughout your day. Try using the same sounds for routine activities to encourage anticipation and imitation.

Your child may not imitate you every time, and that's expected! Hearing your repeated productions helps your child learn sounds and language.

In addition to these sounds, narrate what you do throughout the day in a sing-song way, repeating 2-3 word utterances. For example:

• "Wash, wash, wash hands." During bath time, practice labeling body parts this way. Start with distant body parts to reduce confusion (e.g., hair or head, hands, tummy, feet).
• "Open door," "open mouth," "open book."
• "Push chair in."
• "Light on/off," "coat on/off," "shoe on/off."
• "Clean up, clean up." "Pick up, pick up."
• "Sit down," "get up."
• "Drink, drink, drink milk," "Eat, eat, eat apple."

Notice how speaking in short 2-3 word phrases with repetitions offers your child the next attainable step for verbal imitation.

💡 Studies show that repeatedly labeling a physical object while using or playing with it enhances language acquisition.[2]

Praise your child's attempts to imitate you. "Good talking!" You may try to improve the production if your child is open to it, but attempting to improve every single utterance can cause frustration.

For some, it may be more helpful to designate practice time to two 5-10 minute blocks per day, so your child does not feel overburdened to get their productions correct every time. Provide your child with a reward for their cooperation. You may choose 1-2 "special words" with your SLP that you focus on for a week, giving you permission to prompt your child for improvements at any time. Plan a reward if your child demonstrates improvement with the "special word" over the course of the week. Improvement does not mean perfection, but rather achieving their next attainable step. This may mean just attempting a word approximation.

Every little victory matters. Praise your child for their attempts, their inner motivation, hard work, and specific good habits.
"You are working so hard, and it's showing every day!"
"I love how you focus on my mouth when I move my lips."
"Wow, you made an "O" with your lips just like mommy!"
"Thank you for using your words!"

Consonant and Vowel Sound Combinations

Practice productions at the syllable level since the way we move our articulators to make consonant sounds changes depending on the neighboring vowel. This is called *coarticulation*.

The following pages provide guidance for prompting your child to produce their first functional words.

- Positive repetitions are key to improvement and mastery. Stop when your child is too challenged or is demonstrating frustration.
- Recognize communicative opportunities instead of immediately meeting your child's needs. (e.g., What do you want? (*up, open, go*))
- Be consistent in your new expectations to encourage improvement. Your child is shifting from communicating with gestures (e.g., pointing or grasping towards) and vocalizations (e.g., crying out) to using words paired with new signs/gestures. Encourage your child to at least attempt a word or sign before responding to their request.

💡 *Gesture* refers to an action that can be intuitively understood in most of the world (e.g., nodding head for "yes"). A *Sign* is not universal and may not be intuitively understood (e.g., "nodding" fist up and down for "yes").

pah   poh

Coarticulation: Notice how the lip positioning for the consonant letter /p/ changes depending on the neighboring vowel sound.

Step-by-Step Guidance for Imitation to Independent Productions
Loosely based on the DTTC[3] (Dynamic Temporal and Tactile Cueing) Method

Over time, providing less and less guidance will help your child gain independence with their movements and verbal productions. Start with one syllable words. When your child demonstrates ease with a step over several trials, then move to the next step. Honor your child's pace. With two syllable words, focus on the first syllable before expanding to two.

1. Your child imitates you, as you provide maximal guidance, and bring focus to your mouth while making **slow** exaggerated articulator movements. You may gently position your child's lips and jaw.
   "Watch me, let's do it together!" "Eyes here, then you do!"
   Give specific feedback. *"Nice try, round lips please! Watch, like me!"*

   💡 After each attempted verbal production, show the sign/gesture to build familiarity.

2. Vary how you say the word and invite your child to imitate. Say the word fast and slow. Say it like a question, with excitement, exhaustion, or sadness. Try different sing-song patterns, fast and slow.

3. Silently say the word. Exaggerate the articulator movements, while showing hand cues that bring focus to your mouth, allowing your child to say the word. Finally say the word out-loud again for your child to verbally imitate you with accuracy.
    "Watch me, and you say it! You can do it!"

 If your child cannot achieve this step, move on to another word in order to reduce negative practice. Return to it at another time.

4. Give your child an opportunity to produce the word while you silently say the word and pair it with a familiar sign/gesture.
    "What's the word? You say it, please!"

5. Show your child only the sign/gesture, allowing them to produce the word. (You may cue your child by silently positioning your articulators for the first letter in the word.)
    Ideally, your child will not need verbal encouragement, recognizing the sign/gesture and immediately saying the word with accuracy.

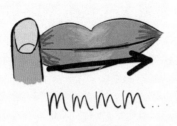

Prompting the reply: Me

Who wants the ball (or other toy, tasty treat, shirt)?
Who wants to go outside (or other favored place)?
Who wants more tickles (or other favored activity or treat)?
Who wants to hide (or play a specific role in a game)?
Who has the shoes (or other object)?
Who popped the bubbles (or completed another activity)?

Take your child's hand and place it on his/her chest when you're prompting the word. Eventually, your child will recognize the gesture when you put your hand on your own chest, and he/she will say "me."

Using a consistent gesture or sign can be a bridge to the verbalized word, and **reduce communicative frustration**. Pairing the physical motion of the sign/gesture with the word can help some children produce the word verbally with increased ease. Studies confirm that teaching a child signs/gestures does not further delay their verbal productions.[4]

Prompting the reply: "ee-ah"/Yah/Yes

"ah" sound as in "ah-pul"/apple

Do you want it?
Do you want more?
Do you want a turn (or specific action in a game - to push, squeeze, throw, put in)?
Do you want to go out (or other favorable activity)?
Did you dance (or other action immediately completed, e.g., drink juice, jump, hug baby)?

If your child is receptively advanced enough and motivated, you may ask about routine activities:
Did you wash your hands?
Did you go potty?
Did you put your toys away?
Did you have fun?

:: "nodding" fist ::

Sign for yes

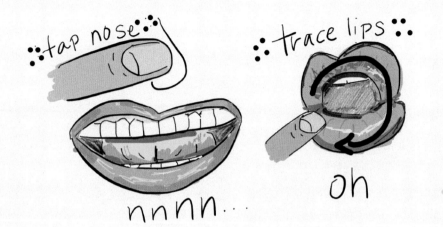

Prompting the reply: No

Intentionally offer an unfavorable choice
or pretend to misunderstand and give
your child the unfavorable choice -
Do you want it?
Other yes/no questions prompting "No":
Do you want more?
Do I put the sock on my ear?
Did you hug the banana (or other
obviously unfavorable/silly action)?

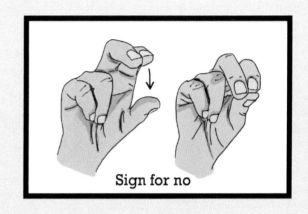

Sign for no

💡 To improve comprehension, ask the question with the referred to object in hand.

Prompting: "ha-ee"/Hi

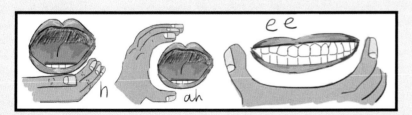

When saying "hi" to
anyone or during pretend
play, pair with a waving
hand gesture.

Prompting the reply: Go

Say, "Ready, set, ..." then wait expectantly for the child to fill in the blank.

When in the car, say "It's green! Let's go!" After modeling "go" in this context several times, wait expectantly for the child to fill in the blank, "It's green! Let's.... "

When playing games like tickling or bouncing on an exercise ball, say "Stop!" and "Go!" to continue the game. Wait expectantly (with an exaggerated facial expression) for the child to say "go" once they understand the pattern in the game.

Sign for go

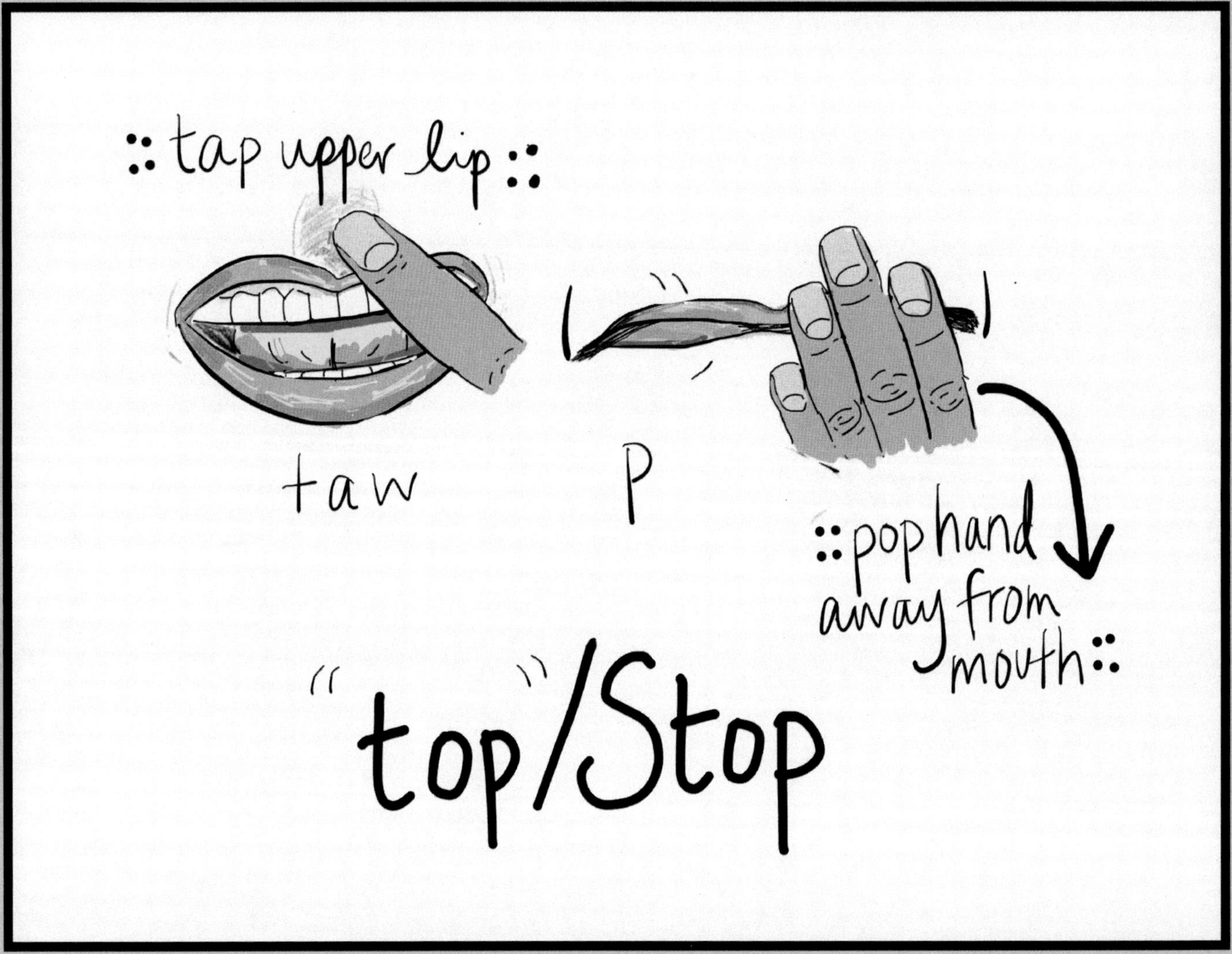
:: tap upper lip ::
taw
p
:: pop hand away from mouth ::
"top/Stop"

Prompting the reply: "dop" or "top"/Stop

The /st/ blend is typically mastered by age 7 for the majority of children.[5]

Play a game where you sing a song, and have a helper model "Stop!" for you to abruptly stop the song, and freeze (make a funny face when you freeze). Your helper then says "Go!" to get you singing again. Your child watches and learns the silly game, eventually saying "Stop!" and "Go!" independently.

While driving, as you approach a red light, say "Goooing to... STOP!" After modeling several repetitions, allow your child to anticipate and fill in the blank, "Goooing to... "

Provide your child with guidance to say, "Stop!" when another child may be trying to take their toy, or play inappropriately with them.

Gesture for stop

Prompting the reply: Up

When your child wants to be picked up, ask, "What do you want?" while you are pointing up to prompt him/her to say "up." Encourage your child to attempt to imitate your production of "up" before completing the action to reinforce expectations.

Model the verbalization, "up, up, up" during pretend play while going up stairs in a doll house. After several repetitions, wait expectantly for your child to say "up" before you complete the action in pretend play.

Do I (throw the ball/blow the bubbles) up or down? (Gesture with your finger pointing up and down.)
Do you want to swing up or stay down? (Exaggerate the words "up" and "down" in the question.)
Where are you going? (On a playground ladder or stairs.)
Where is the (airplane/bird/squirrel)?

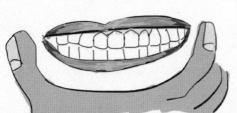

eee...

::tap upper lip::

t

Eat

::Bring pinched hand to mouth::

Prompting the reply: Eat

When your child is about to eat, say "Time to eat" while showing the gesture. After several repetitions, say "Time to … " and wait expectantly while bringing focus to your mouth shaped for the long "EE" sound and/or while showing the sign.

Create a routine in pretend play, say "siiiiit doooown (in a sing-song voice stretching out the vowels), eat, eat, eat." After several repetitions, invite your child to fill in the blank by waiting expectantly, "siiiiit doooown… " then wait expectantly for your child to say "eat" before you complete the pretend feeding action.

💡 Celebrate any production your child attempts. Invite your child to improve their production. (e.g. ,"Nice try, so close! One more time, big smile, teeth together for the EEE.. sound.")

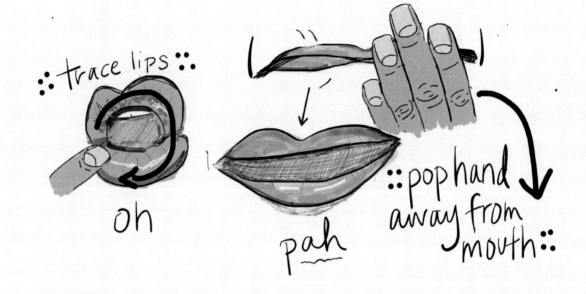

trace lips

oh

pah

pop hand away from mouth

"Oh-pah"/Open

Prompting the reply: "oh-pah"/Open

Once your child can easily produce the approximation, then focus on final consonant inclusion.

Ask "What do I do with it?" when you:
Open a door in the house or the car door.
Open a seat belt.
Open the top of any container
(e.g., bubbles, juice, play-doh).
Open a ziplock bag (you may
pretend to pour out the contents
while the bag is still sealed shut).
Open a book.
Open a game box, or any part of the
game that requires the child to open
something.

Sign for open

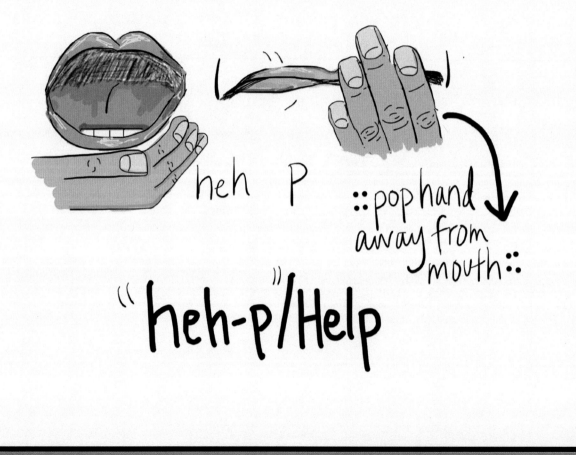

Prompting the reply: "heh-p"/Help

Anytime your child is giving you an object for assistance or is producing vocalizations and reaching to request help, use the motivated opportunity. If your child's request is not urgent, and he/she has the patience at the time to focus, work on producing at least a verbal approximation "heh" or "heh-p." If that's too challenging, put your hands on your child's hands to assist him/her in showing you the sign for "help" before completing the request.

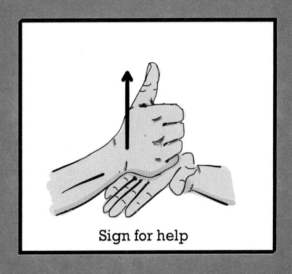

Sign for help

Once your child is able to say, "help" and "me" when cued with a sign and gesture, you can extend to the two word phrase, "Help me."

"mo"/More in a Two Word Phrase

Some SLPs introduce the word and sign for "more" as one of the first words during early intervention since it includes early developing bilabial sound /m/ and is easy to apply to a variety of activities. However, this can actually be a frustrating word and sign to teach since a child may overgeneralize and a caregiver may not understand what the child specifically wants.

Sign for more

It's a great word to introduce once a child has some other words first (e.g. eat, milk, favorite foods, favorite activity) to produce a two word phrase. Eventually you can add "I want" to create a four word request phrase (e.g, I want more bubble).

Prompting the reply: "mo"/More + (desired object)

Do you want more? Tell me:
(prompt the word "more" or sign) + (prompt the word for desired object/activity)

☐ Expand to the 2 word phrase when your child can easily produce at least a word approximation for the desired object/activity.

"poo"/Poop

Poop can be one of the most motivating words for children. Until your child is able to consistently produce the word, the sign can be helpful in potty training. When prompting your child to say the word, show the sign as well. You may help your child form the sign with their own hand by providing hand-over-hand guidance.

Sign for poop

"wah"/Want

Produce a soft final consonant /t/, not an exaggerated "tah" sound.

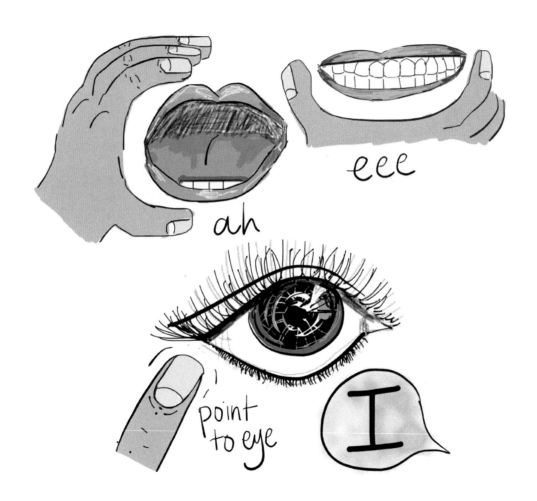

Requesting & Expanding to Two to Four Word Phrases

"Wah"/Want + (desired activity/object)
"Ah-ee"/I + "wah"/want + (desired activity/object)
"Ah-ee"/I + "wah"/want + "mo"/more + (desired activity/object)

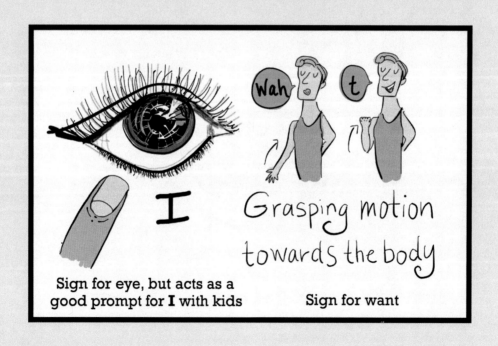

Sign for eye, but acts as a
good prompt for **I** with kids

Sign for want

TOOL KIT

A Letter for your Child's Classmates

Parents may feel anxious about how their child will make friends in school. Children are more open when they understand why a peer is different. You may consider sending a note home with your child's classmates so parents can encourage their child to be understanding and accepting when they meet someone who speaks differently than they do. Feel free to use these letters and edit to personalize them for your child.

Dear Friend,

I am excited to meet you! I want to share that I talk a little differently and sometimes it's hard to understand what I'm saying. Sometimes, it's tricky for me to move my mouth like I want to and say my words clearly, but I'm working hard to get better. I can understand all your words. I'd like to be friends with you, play games, and learn with you. Thank you for your kindness!

Your friend,
(Your child's name)

Dear Parent,

I'd like to share with you that my son/daughter, (Name), is diagnosed with a(n) (expressive language disorder/speech sound disorder/Childhood Apraxia of Speech) and is currently receiving speech-language therapy to improve the intelligibility of his/her speech. He/she is bright, playful, and kind, but sometimes other children aren't sure how to interact with him/her because his/her speech isn't always clear. I trust that increasing understanding can positively influence (Name)'s preschool experience, and help build empathy in his/her classmates. I sincerely appreciate you speaking to your child about (Name)'s speech challenges and desire for connection. (Name) understands others and is excited to make new friends. If you'd like to learn more about (expressive language delays, please visit http://tinyurl.com/explanguage*/ speech sound disorders, please visit http://tinyurl.com/speechsounddisorders*/ Childhood Apraxia of Speech, please visit www.apraxia-kids.com). Thank you for your help in making this a socially successful year for my child! Please feel free to contact me if you have questions.

With Gratitude,
(parent's name and contact information)

---

* These shortened web addresses are directed to the American Speech Language and Hearing Association.

You may also consider sending a letter to your child's teacher. This letter is provided by the website www.Apraxia-Kids.org. Although it was written with Childhood Apraxia of Speech in mind, the list of ways the teacher can support your child can be valuable for other communicative diagnoses as well:

https://www.apraxia-kids.org/wp-content/uploads/2013/01/Letter-To-A-Teacher.pdf

These letters also available with active links on the website www.MehreenKakwan.com

FLASH CARDS

After you cut out the flashcards on the following pages, you may choose to laminate or glue them to thicker card stock to increase durability.

Please note that if your child is having difficulty understanding picture symbols, they may need to develop pre-verbal skills before flashcards can be effective.

The functional words offered here are abstract as they don't link to real objects.

"ee-ah"/Yes

Me

No

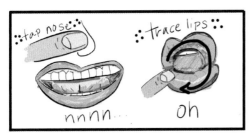

Go

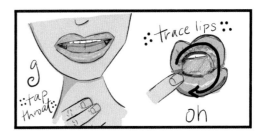

"top"/Stop

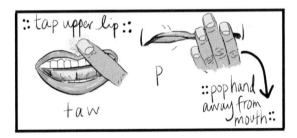

:: tap upper lip ::

taw

P

:: pop hand away from mouth ::

Up

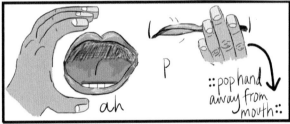

ah

P

:: pop hand away from mouth ::

Eat

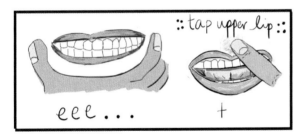

eee . . .   :: tap upper lip ::   +

"oh-pah"/Open

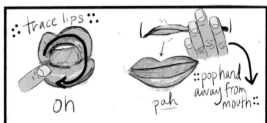

:: trace lips ::   oh   pah   :: pop hand away from mouth ::

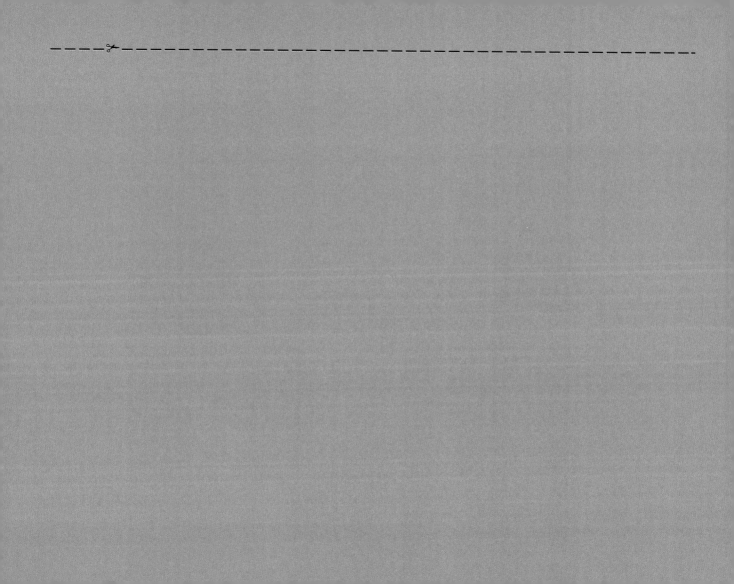

"mo"/More

trace lips

mmm...

"heh-p"/Help

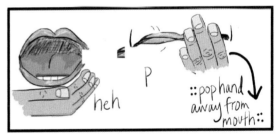

heh

P

pop hand away from mouth

"ha-ee"/Hi

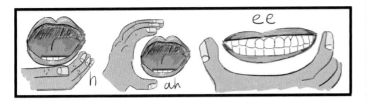

"wah"/Want

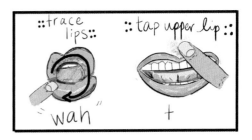

Notes

Please visit www.MehreenKakwan.com for a page of active website links to these references

1. Laura Mize, "Milestones," *Teach Me To Talk: Helping Parents Teach Toddlers to Understand and Use Language*. (2019) Retrieved from http://teachmetotalk.com/
2. Clerkin Elizabeth M.,,et al. "Real-world visual statistics and infants' first-learned object names," *Philosophical Transactions of the Royal Society B: Biological Sciences* no. 1711 (2017): http://doi.org/10.1098/rstb.2016.0055.
3. Strand, Edythe. "Integral Stimulation Method (Adapted for Children as DTTC)." *Apraxia Kids Newsletter*, June 2005, http://www.apraxia-kids.org/apraxia_kids_library/integral-stimulation-method-adapted-for-children-as-dttc/.
4. Dunst, Carl J., Meter Diana, Hamby, Deborah W. "Influences of sign and oral language interventions on the speech and oral language production of young children with disabilities," *Center for Early Literacy Learning,* no. 4 (2011): http://earlyliteracylearning.org/cellreviews/cellreviews_v4_n4.pdf
5. Smit, A B, et al. "The Iowa Articulation Norms Project and Its Nebraska Replication." *The Journal of Speech and Hearing Disorders*, U.S. National Library of Medicine, Nov. 1990, www.ncbi.nlm.nih.gov/pubmed/2232757

———

Recommended Online Resources for Families

http://slpmommyofapraxia.com - Resources and support from an SLP and mother of a child with CAS
https://teachmetotalk.com - Great resource for pre-verbal skills and helping delayed talkers.
   - Also, "Teach Me To Talk" on YouTube for helpful videos to assist delayed talkers
https://www.cariebertseminars.com - Geared towards SLPs, however families can benefit from her toy list and her new product, environmental/animal sound picture cards to help build imitation skills

ABOUT THE AUTHOR

Mehreen Kakwan is an ASHA (American Speech-Language and Hearing Association) certified speech-language pathologist with a passion for being a catalyst for positive growth and healing. She earned her Master's in Speech-Language Pathology at Eastern Michigan University, and her Bachelor's of Science in Economics and Pre-med at The University of Michigan - Ann Arbor. Inspired by her patient's healing journeys, she combined her love for illustrating and writing with her desire to help more children feel a sense of belonging, self-acceptance and hope. Mehreen lives in Ann Arbor, Michigan.

Photo by Katelyn Wollet | www.katelynwollet.com

Made in the USA
Middletown, DE
02 June 2021